Simple Joys

Reflections on Life's Little Miracles

Kathleen McDonald

Copyright © 2017 Kathleen McDonald.

All rights reserved. No part of this book may be used or reproduced by any means, graphic, electronic, or mechanical, including photocopying, recording, taping or by any information storage retrieval system without the written permission of the publisher except in the case of brief quotations embodied in critical articles and reviews.

NIV -Scripture quotations marked (NIV) are taken from the Holy Bible, New International Version®, NIV®. Copyright © 1973, 1978, 1984, 2011 by Biblica, Inc.™ Used by permission of Zondervan. All rights reserved worldwide.

***

RSV - Scripture quotations marked (RSV) are from the Revised Standard Version of the Bible, copyright © 1946, 1952, and 1971 National Council of the Churches of Christ in the United States of America. Used by permission. All rights reserved.

WestBow Press books may be ordered through booksellers or by contacting:

WestBow Press
A Division of Thomas Nelson & Zondervan
1663 Liberty Drive
Bloomington, IN 47403
www.westbowpress.com
1 (866) 928-1240

Revised Standard Version of the Bible, copyright ©1952 [2nd edition, 1971] by the Division of Christian Education of the National Council of the Churches of Christ in the United States of America. Used by permission. All rights reserved.

Because of the dynamic nature of the Internet, any web addresses or links contained in this book may have changed since publication and may no longer be valid. The views expressed in this work are solely those of the author and do not necessarily reflect the views of the publisher, and the publisher hereby disclaims any responsibility for them.

Any people depicted in stock imagery provided by Thinkstock are models, and such images are being used for illustrative purposes only. Certain stock imagery © Thinkstock.

ISBN: 978-1-9736-0919-3 (sc)
ISBN: 978-1-9736-0920-9 (hc)
ISBN: 978-1-9736-0918-6 (e)

Library of Congress Control Number: 2017917999

Print information available on the last page.

WestBow Press rev. date: 2/7/2018

Dedication

For my sons: Michael, who often calls me Swami San, and Justin, who tries to teach me math. Both of you hold a special place in my heart. God's blessings, you handsome dudes.

Contents

Dedication v
Preface ix
Acknowledgments xi

Part 1 Stories of Faithfulness

In the Footsteps of Abraham 2
    Prayer 8
    Poem: A Gentle Nudge 9

Faithful Max and the Miracle Lady 11
    Prayer 18
    Poem: Saint Bernard Buddy 19

Part 2 Stories of Humor

God's Sense of Humor 24
    Prayer 30
    Poem: Travel Friend 31

The Chimney Monster 33
    Prayer 38
    Poem: Laughter 39

Part 3 Stories of Perseverance

The Report 44
    Prayer 56
    Poem: Gift 57

A Gentle Gift 59
    Prayer 66
    Poem: Challenge 67

Part 4 Stories of Joy

The Miracle Maple 72
    Prayer 77
    Poem: Tree Treasure 78

A Small Miracle 80
    Prayer 84
    Poem: Needlework 85

Part 5 Stories of Awareness

Boxes of Memories 90
    Prayer 94
    Poem: Masterpiece 95

My Father's Arms 97
    Prayer 101
    Poem: Simple Games 102

Afterword 107
About the Author 109

Preface

My first book, *Simpler Times: Reflections on Women's Friendship*, dealt with a specific group of women who touched my life. However, there are so many stories in my life and so much more to share that my first book needed a companion. You, my readers, had asked for more, and your enthusiasm inspired me to look over my voluminous files of writing and poetry. In the process I laughed and shed a tear or two revisiting my own life stories as well as the stories of those close to me. Many wonderful adventures that inspired me in the past came forward as the springboard for this book.

Life is such a journey, and each road we take can teach us something. We learn and grow and learn and grow again—straight roads and curvy, narrow lanes and broad vistas, bumps in the road and even an occasional pothole. Life is a mosaic of adventures.

Curiously, this book took on a life of its own. About halfway through its pages, I realized that it was teaching *me* as I wrote. I had started with the idea of sharing journeys that had changed me in some way, but the Holy Spirit within invited me along another path. I discovered that most of the stories involved simple miracles, those touch-of-life miracles that happen so often in our lives that we may not always see them as such. With awesome delight, I found an inner joy in the telling, a *gift miracle* for my soul. Then, as I reviewed each story, I realized what amazing insights surface when the Lord is the writing guide.

My dad once sagely reminded me that each stage in life offers new challenges that increase our wisdom. He said to look for the treasure waiting to be discovered. I remember this advice often. The adventure of writing this book was nurtured by his never-stop-growing philosophy. Looking at my personal stories in new ways, I have gleaned much from the garden of my life. In the pages that follow, I hope you will share my delight and that, again, your hearts will swell with joy.

Finally, be aware of miracles; they are around you every day.

(I've presented the stories in sets of two because I felt they fit together in theme and purpose. Enjoy!)

—Kathy McDonald

Acknowledgments

So many people helped me write this book—some with nitty-gritty work and some with encouragement. The Dippy Dabblers, my painting, card-making, and friendship group, who, after lovingly helping me launch my first book, have readily accepted my absence as I've worked on this one. My Wednesday Women in the Word Bible study group, who support me daily with prayer and encouragement. My water aerobics pals who thrilled me with their support for my first book and are anticipating its companion. My dear family, and my husband, Dick, who wonders if I will ever retire and watch the grass grow. (I told him I would retire at eighty-four, so why does he keep asking me?)

My dear sister, Anita Jacobs, who is a wonderful editor—I so enjoy discussing sentence structure and the many theories about the use of commas with her. Ginny Gallagher, who does my technical editing and challenges me to defend an idea or two. Carol von Hagn, who enjoys my writing and gently offers ideas for change. My daughter, Becky Diette, who willingly read and helped edit despite her busy schedule homeschooling a large family.

And of course all the other friends and groups who have been so supportive and given me the courage to forge ahead.

Part 1

Stories of Faithfulness

In the Footsteps of Abraham

> Leave your country and your people and your father's household and go to the land I will show you.
>
> —Genesis 12:1 (RSV)

The year that Justin, my youngest, started kindergarten was a year of great change in our family. My husband chose to leave our family and go his own way. By God's grace, this new path in my life started in the cocoon of the wonderful women you may have met in *Simpler Times: Reflections on Women's Friendship*. God used them to make a butterfly out of me and prepare me to fly. I was ready for whatever He had in store for my children and me.

During that year, I spent time praying and putting out feelers for possible jobs. I babysat, worked with Head Start, and took courses to add an extra certification to my teaching degree, which gave me more options in applying for jobs.

I look back on that time with amazement and thanksgiving, recalling the stubbornness of my resolve to wait for the Lord. I wanted clear direction. He honored my intentions by reassuring me through so many little miracles. The kids and I nurtured each other in our brokenness, and all of our friends supported us with their time, loving-kindness, and willingness to listen. When I needed something—even something as simple as apples for my kids' lunches—there would be a knock on the door and one of our friends would smile and say, "I felt led to bring you a bag of apples." Sometimes it was a meal: "I woke up this morning and knew that you needed supper tonight, and here it is." Friends provided rides, as I had no car, and they offered us help with warm clothing as well as constant prayer and encouragement. I will spend my whole life paying it forward for all that was done to help us during that year.

One time, when we had a deep freeze in our area, I heard our pipes banging away. We had an old Victorian Queen Anne–style house with one of those cold, open cellars. I was sure I'd have no water in the morning and no way to fix the problem. I pulled the blankets over my head and fell into a fitful sleep.

In the morning, I walked to the bathroom expecting the inevitable. Lo and behold, nothing had frozen, though many of our neighbors had experienced bursting pipes. I believed then, as I do now, that the Lord was my plumber, albeit a noisy one, taking care of His little family. He knew our needs and provided.

Time passed with no clear direction. Then I got a letter from Barbara, a teacher I had worked with before I was married. She knew that I was looking for a job and apologized that there was nothing available. However, she mentioned in passing a part-time position at the little

Christian school where she taught; it would just be for a few hours a day. I felt compelled to call her.

When I told her why I was calling, she was astonished. She didn't remember writing anything about this *phantom* job. I had to read the letter to her before she would believe me. (I'm sure you know what I thought about it.) In the end, she told me she would talk to her sister, the principal.

The principal called me a day or two later. She remembered me from the time I worked with Barbara and had been impressed with my teaching. She actually *had* been thinking of hiring someone to help out part-time in the fall and said she would love to have me on her staff. However, she sighed, "I cannot offer more than part-time. You are a year too early. Our board has been talking about adding another grade the following fall." Then she threw out a wistful wish that perhaps I could find a second job and take her part-time offering in September. Then, in the next school year, she would hire me full time in a minute.

I hung up, befuddled. It made no sense, but it felt just right—I knew it. What a ludicrous thought! A part-time job? A new town over two hours away? I needed time to think and pray. Of all the inquiries I had going back and forth, this one seemed to nudge at my heart. Of course, it was illogical to move to a new town for a part-time job.

When the Lord says, "Go!" He does not relent. The positives and negatives went down on paper. The negatives included sadness at leaving my dear friends, my lack of money and the promise of little more, and no idea where I would live. But on the other hand, I had the strong feeling of peacefulness that accompanies the still, small voice of the Lord and the prospect of being closer to my family, who would be about thirty miles away. In fact, my sister, who was recently widowed, understood my faith in following the Lord. She invited us to live with her family while I looked for a place of our own and that elusive second job. After much soul searching, I called and accepted this new challenge.

In the following months, I saved every cent I could. The children and I planned a moving sale at which I sold anything we didn't need from our home. Then, with a promise of help with the packing and driving, I rented a U-Haul truck and prepared to go to a new town with $1,200, four children, a guinea pig, a cat, a part-time job, no car, and a load of faith.

Twenty-seven people came to help me pack up and fill the truck. It was happy bedlam. There were cars up and down the street, and the Lord put His hedge of protection around us. They chased me out of the house and sat me down in a rocking chair on Grace's porch across the street.

Grace, dear friend that she is (the coffee lady in *Simpler Times*), and Lilly, a gal who always offers everything to God's honor and glory, volunteered to support me through the trip. So the next day, Sophie, my wise friend (see *Simpler Times*), took the kids while the three of us took off on this new adventure. Grace drove (my driving is suspect), Lilly encouraged, and I navigated.

We had such an amazing trip. We were a live-action, road-trip movie, moving hesitantly along the road. Like the Three Stooges from the long-ago comedy shorts, we had never checked the gas gauge before we left. We chugged to the top of a high hill literally on fumes. We needed gas—and right away! Happily, a gas station grinned at us just as we huffed up the last portion of the hill. Laughing with a mixture of anxiety and relief, we coasted up to a gas pump. Naturally, none of us had ever attempted putting gas in such a big, old truck, but we garnered the courage to give the self-serve pump a try. Successful, we lumbered back onto the road.

God had obviously been protecting us because if we hadn't stopped for gas, we would have been involved in an accident ahead. We thanked the Lord as we passed the two cars we'd previously been shadowing in a multicar pileup. Our gas gauge had saved us from harm. We passed the area, which was by then surrounded by blinking lights and much turmoil, and prayed for those involved.

Grace, Lilly, and I continued on, soon returning from that somber moment to our good humor. We wondered what would come next. Finally we arrived at my new village. I had no idea where the school was, so the three of us had to find it as well as the home of the sisters who were not only waiting for our arrival but also providing a storage area for my furniture. (I laugh whenever I think of the chance I took. It was truly a leap of faith.)

We stopped and asked a random passerby where the Christian school was. "Well," she said, "it is one street over and about where you are right now." Surprise, surprise! It was a nice-looking, two-story, golden-brick elementary school—and right down the street we easily found the house of my new principal and her sister.

With butterflies swirling in my stomach, I walked up the sidewalk and knocked. The door opened, and a sweet little lady welcomed me. Instead of greeting me with a smile, she looked so serious that I took pause. She said, "Did you find a job to complement your position here?"

"No, not yet," I replied. Now I had a sinking feeling in my stomach.

"We had an emergency meeting of our school board this morning." She paused as my inside butterflies multiplied. "We decided unanimously to add a grade level to our school this September. We will have a sixth grade, and we would like to hire you for a full-time position."

Hugs! Tears, laughter, and joy! I had dared to take that first step, and He had provided the plan. My moving party and I jumped and danced with joy.

So here I am! The children and I went to school together for those first transition years, I met my dear husband at a Bible study, and I went on to teach in a public school when this dear little school was closed.

What a witness this has been for me over the years. Whenever I am faced with a near-impossible situation, I am reminded of God's faithfulness and know that God will take my hand if I try to walk on the water.

> He [Jesus] said, "Come." So Peter got out of the boat and walked on the water and came to Jesus." (Matthew 14:29 RSV)

Prayer

Dear Lord, there are times when You call us to get out of the boat and walk with You on the water. I wonder how often we miss them because of uncertainty and fear. It is so easy to stay fixed and just let adventures pass us by. It's much easier to be secure, too risky to take that new fork in the road.

Lord, help me to hear Your voice calling me to follow You. When You call me forth, help me not to hold on to the safety of the boat but know that You will never abandon me, no matter how deep the water seems. Amen

A Gentle Nudge

Lord,
Today on my windy walk,
You pushed me from behind
And took me down the path you'd planned for me,
With little love taps of wind gusts
Reminding me
That You will take me where I should go
If I just trust.

Faithful Friend

Faithful Max and the Miracle Lady

They who wait upon the Lord shall renew their strength; they shall mount up with wings like eagles; they shall run and not be weary; they shall walk and not faint.

—Isaiah 40:31 (RSV)

When my daughter, Melissa, moved to New Mexico, she took only the basic necessities and left most of her treasures at home. So, when she bought her little house, she asked if Mom and Dad could possibly bring the bulk of her lifelong accumulations to her southwestern home. We were excited at the prospect of an across-country road trip and gladly agreed.

While we were making our plans, I just happened to win a beautiful rocking chair at a church bazaar, which I knew Missy would love. So, much to the chagrin of my husband, I added the chair to the myriad of items I had gathered to put in our four-door sedan.

I was busy with last-minute packing when my husband came in and said, "We will never fit all of this stuff into our vehicle." I walked out to see what the problem seemed to be and saw the futility of that packing job.

"Just give me a few minutes to think," I said. No sooner had the words left my mouth than I had my answer: "Take it all out, and I will use the Nifty Natalie method of packing this car."

My friend Natalie is the most organized person I have ever known. We worked together for several years, and her classroom was always "well groomed." At the end of the school day, my desk looked like impending doom, and her desk would have a few papers and possibly a paper clip out of place. The reality of the state of my room after teaching contrasted sharply with *her* totally outrageous exclamation, "My room is a mess!"

Nat's messy desk was nothing in comparison to her storage closets. In all my years, I have never met anyone who could fit so much into a small space *and* know what was in each inch of those crowded closets. I watched in amazement as supply after supply would somehow gracefully fit here or there.

So, with stubborn determination, I challenged myself to pack that car just like Natalie would. I put on my "Nat hat" and willed my brain to step into hers and get the job done. I used Dick for the heavy lifting, but I tackled that car like it was an Olympic event. I moved, squeezed, and piled things. Finally, the task was done. I stood back and evaluated it to see if Natalie would approve. My alternate personality had fit every single parcel, package, suitcase, crate, and book into that car, as well as the rocking chair, which sat precariously tilted in the back seat. The car sighed under the weight, and I think I heard a groan emanate from within. So, thanks to Natalie, we went off to New Mexico in a vehicle that any covered-wagon train would have approved of.

So what does this have to do with miracles? Well, this same Natalie is a walking miracle who, unbeknownst to her, taught me not only how to pack but also much about surviving against all odds. From her first diagnosis of cancer over twelve years ago, she has overcome three types of cancer and several near-death experiences resulting from the ravages of her battle to survive.

Natalie's first bout with cancer was sudden and unexpected. It came as a shock, and the road ahead included surgery, chemotherapy, and radiation. The course of treatment as well as choosing the right doctors and best treatment center was overwhelming. As her friend, I wanted to be there for her in any way I could.

Having recently retired, I considered subbing for her, but I didn't feel at peace with that choice. Instead, I had the strong feeling that I would serve her better as a support person. Her husband was working, and her daughters were busy, one in college and the other involved with high school activities. Finally, Natalie, her husband, and I sat down and devised a plan: she would take the year off, and I would be her go-to person for the days she would need transportation to the treatment center, as well as other needs she might have. We prayed and, feeling at peace, decided to start this blessed and hope-filled journey together.

A few days later, Nat called me in tears. "Oh, Kathy, you won't believe what my girls did. I don't know what to do. They bought me a Saint Bernard puppy to keep me company. How could they?"

"Well, at least they didn't buy you a coffin," I replied in my wry manner.

"Ohhh!" she moaned and then started to laugh. A new challenge was thrown into the mix. Natalie was good with dogs, so I saw this as a gift to keep her mind busy as she trained him. Little did I know that I, who had never owned a dog, was about to become the auntie of a wonderfully frisky, drooling, *big,* and curious creature.

Natalie and I started our almost daily trips to the cancer center where she courageously endured an intense program. With her droll sense of humor and my madcap nonsense, we kept the waiting room laughing. I remember several times people came up and asked us how we maintained such a good attitude. We would then share a few positive words to grateful ears. Within God's grace, we were a perfect fit, helping many in those little ways that count.

The treatments were relentless and extremely debilitating for Natalie. It wasn't all laughter, of course. We cried together and prayed together often. Sometimes words were not needed. We grew to know and understand each other, as well as support each other. I learned that both caregiver and patient discover valuable truths from each other, and I believe the growth we experienced had an impact on how God molded us for the future. It was a devastating yet grace-filled time.

And then there was Max the dog. Before we left for any appointment, we had to tend to the puppy. I learned to walk a dog—often a comedy of errors, as this young pup's goal in life was to sample new things, especially in the area of outdoor food experimentation. It was quite a job keeping him away from the castoffs that people had thrown here and there.

In the beginning of her treatments, Natalie walked with us and trained Max and me. As time passed, she became weaker and I became this growing puppy's morning walking companion. Saint Bernards, even when little, are pretty hefty, and more than once he frisked off to investigate something new, pulling me along behind him. When chastened, he would turn those soulful eyes on me, making me feel that I was the one who had strayed from the path. And, of course, he loved me and showed his love with nice, drippy saliva kisses or wet toy offerings. Along with his friendly nature, he just grew and grew.

What started as a potential disaster turned out to be just what the doctor ordered because Nat loved that big, old bruiser. I learned dogs are truly loyal creatures that are very forgiving of people who do not know what they are doing (could that have been me?). His silly antics gave Natalie the gift of laughter as she sat exhausted in her cozy chair. And Max actually *sat* on the couch, which was close to her. He would back up and sit down just like a human. It was a funny sight to see, though somewhat traumatic as Max got bigger and bigger. We wondered if he thought he was just one of us.

Natalie was and still is a strong woman of quiet faith. No cancer was going to defeat her. She set a goal to visit her daughter at college by Thanksgiving *no matter what*. That prayer was answered as she finished her last treatment just before the holiday. Though exhausted, she and her husband went to see their girl.

That wonderful Saint Bernard stayed with Natalie through two more types of cancer, which she boldly conquered. He got so big that when he stood on my foot, I thought it would break. But he warmed and blessed her while she blessed others with her gift of acceptance and gutsy determination.

Sweet, furry Max is now buried in her backyard with my memorial variegated hosta growing nearby. I grew to love him—a striking example of how dog companions can give faithful love and encouragement to their masters.

When Natalie went back to work the next year, the children learned, through her subsequent cancers, what it is like to serve while suffering. The staff supported her with wonderful school fund-raisers for cancer victims. Others who know her and face cancer take inspiration from her example. It is unquestionable that she taught me a great deal, and I count those times with her as some of the most memorable of my life.

Natalie goes on stubbornly fighting a different battle nowadays. She is dealing with the radiation effects of that first cancer. She has been in and out of the hospital for more than a year and, at times, near death. Retired now, she is learning to live a new life with multiple complications.

Her husband valiantly cares for her, and she still has dog companions—but none can replace that big Max.

I have no idea where Natalie's new path will take her, but I do know that she is an inspiration to many people. Her example teaches that we can survive through many dark days with the Lord's help and come out into the sun of joy. Natalie is a ray of hope and sunshine to all who know her.

> And after you have suffered for a little while, the God of all grace, who has called you to His eternal glory in Christ, will himself restore, establish, and strengthen you. (1Peter 5:10 RSV)

Prayer

Lord, *cancer* is a dreaded word, a dreaded diagnosis. Few families escape it. It has no regard for our plans, hopes, and dreams. Suddenly, pushed out of a safe world, one feels underwater, struggling toward the surface, abandoned and lost. But You reach down to take our hands. You pull us up just in time and shelter us in Your arms. You are here.

Help those, Lord, who are plagued with this mysterious foe to hear Your voice. Help those who agonize over a loved one who has been asked to bear this cross. Help them to trust faithfully in Your will, a will we often do not understand, Amen

Saint Bernard Buddy

Round, soft, furry friend,
No alpine snow-filled mountains here
Yet you still bring that spirit of hope,
A keg of life-giving water,
Your instinctual self.
Abiding, drooling, monster dog,
Loving
Caring
Spread out by your lady's chair,
keeping feet warm with soft-haired coat.
You amble precariously through the house
(who knows what you will break?)
Then dance down the road, pulling powerfully.
You cannot help but bring a smile,
a healing balm
to a fragile fighting-for-life figure.

Questions to Contemplate or Discuss:

1. In the first story, the author stepped out in faith. Think of a time when you were placed in a position where God was asking you to take a first step out of your safety zone. Share what happened.
2. The author felt like an Abraham when she moved. What Bible story do you identify with in relation to an event in your own life.
3. Share a hopeful story about your bout with cancer and/or a story about a cancer patient dear to you.

Scripture Readings and Reflections:

Genesis 12
James 11
Psalm 34

Books to Read:

For courage:
Do It Afraid by Joyce Meyer
Number the Stars by Lois Lowry
The Hiding Place by Corrie Ten Boom

For dog lovers:

The Dog Who Wouldn't Be by Farley Mowat (It will make you laugh.)

A Big Little Life: A Memoir of a Joyful Dog Named Trixie by Dean Koontz

Natalie suggests: *A Dog's Purpose* by W. Bruce Cameron

Personal Reflections:

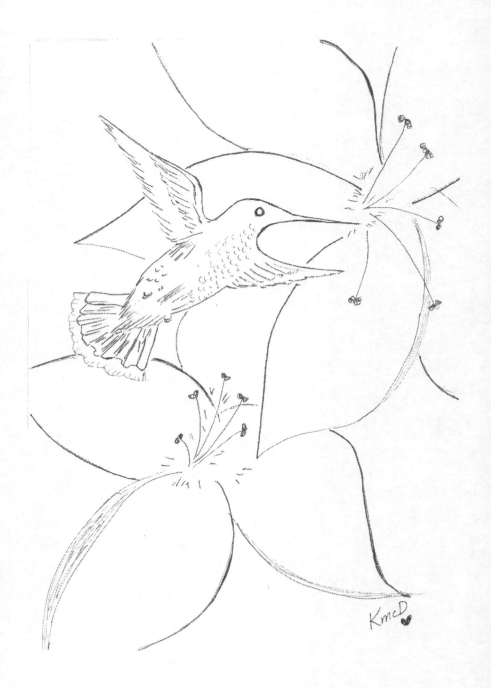

Part 2

Stories of Humor

God's Sense of Humor

Oh! Send out Your light and Your truth; let them lead me. Let them bring me to Your holy hill and to your dwelling place.

—Psalm 43:3 (RSV)

Then our mouth was filled with laughter, and our tongue with shouts of joy.

—Psalm 126:2 (RSV)

Knowing with wonder and thanksgiving that I *really* had a *full-time* job, my children and I settled into the summer, living with my dear sister until I could find a place to rent. She graciously welcomed us into her family. To help pay our share of the living expenses, I babysat for her while she worked. With my four mischief makers and her three angels, we enjoyed a truly memorable time, e.g., hitting baseballs through windows; getting bathed, seven at a time, with a hose in the backyard; stopping to count to be sure all seven were with us; and watching *Monster Matinee* on Saturday afternoons and my sister's sleek, black Burmese cat staring down our huge, old, mongrel tiger cat.

During my free time, I scoured the ads from the Bath area for a place to live. It seemed that reasonably priced rental homes for single parents were few and far between. I prayed that God would find a little place for us to live with a little space to grow flowers. He faithfully answered my little prayer by sending me to look at several small places in the village. I especially remember the two smallest.

The first little house was shaped like a rectangle with three tiny bedrooms hardly big enough for bunks. The kitchen, living room, and dining room combination was the size of a normal bathroom. The bathroom was the size of a closet. While it *was* a cozy little place, I would have had to install a traffic light so the kids and I could move without running into each other. Even with a traffic light, I think bodily injury would have been a daily given. There also was a tiny area outside the front door where I might have been able to plant some tulips, but that was it. My family was bigger than the house.

The other place I remember fondly. It was one of the loveliest little houses I have ever seen. It was like a dollhouse with a white picket fence and window boxes perfect for flowers. It was a Cape-Cod style with shutters and a tiny breakfast nook near a lace-curtained window. The girl who lived there was single and about the same size as my eight-year-old. It was the tiniest, sweetest little place—the perfect playhouse for my girls. The five of us, however, would have literally burst its seams.

After I walked out of that dollhouse and got into my car, I put my hands on the steering wheel and laughed. "I get the joke, Lord. You're having fun with me." As you can see, He *had* answered my prayer. Every one of the many places we saw were little, and each one had a place to plant flowers. In His sense of humor, the Lord was putting me on while challenging me to ask for what I *really* needed,

Our home In Central New York had had thirteen *big* rooms. We had a huge vegetable garden, two flower gardens, and a big yard. When I said "little" in my prayer, the meaning in my mind was "little in comparison." Needless to say, I reworded my prayer: "Lord, what we need is a house that is the right size for us—a house with enough room to move around—and yes, I'd still like to plant some flowers there."

The next house I saw was just what we needed. It seemed like a half-size model of our previous home. It even had an upstairs porch where I could pray at night before bed (one of the features of our Victorian that I had loved). The rent was higher than I'd hoped and would mean a struggle for me financially, but I trusted that, because it was an answered prayer, I would be able to pull it off. We couldn't move in until November, but the extra time gave me a chance to take in a few paychecks and save for the rent.

The house had some funny quirks. The kitchen's water pipes were on the outside wall in the back of the house. This meant that every cold day the water would freeze. The previous renters had shown me their hidden path to the frozen-pipe problem. Under the sink there was a hole, and they told me to use a hair dryer to unfreeze the water. Problem solved.

The upstairs was so cold in the winter that one night the wallpaper just sighed and separated itself from the wall. It never fell off; it just kind of lingered there. We quickly learned the skillful use of multiple blanketing.

The plumbing was archaic, and I bought a poster from the Boynton Collection that stated, "I march to the *pound* of a distant plumber," as the plunger became my very close friend. (Sometimes I must admit this problem was anything but funny.)

However, God still continued to engage me with humor. Across the street from us lived an eccentric little old lady. She was a noted community icon, and most people steered clear of her because she had been known to attack people with brooms and even frying pans. I knew little about our new community, but I'd heard plenty of stories about her from my sister and her friends. The woman was not fond of children. Naturally, one of the first things my kids decided to do was to take ripe cherries off her cherry tree. Out she came, not pleased. She walked across the street like a storm cloud with little rivulets of steam seeping out of her ears. I smiled hesitantly and listened. By the end of our conversation, she had evaluated and accepted me. I would like to think that she saw the light of the Lord through me. In any case, she visited with us quite often and shared some of her life with us. She was a masterful gardener although, true to her nature, she planted things in unusual places. I loved looking at her feast of flowers.

I am not sure if she chose to be a recluse or if it was

because most people were so afraid of her. I do know that she stood guard over my children and me; she came flying out to protect them anytime she saw a potential problem.

After we moved away from that neighborhood and before she died, I would see her occasionally here and there. As she aged, she was not sure who I was anymore. But she would always point at me with a smile and say, "I know you." I sure was grateful that she liked me!

We stayed in that old house until the girl who lived next door helped me find another house with lower rent and a large play area for the kids. That move brought us joyous discoveries as well as new hardships—but so it is with life.

During this little slice of my life, I learned lessons of generosity from my sister and of the effect of showing love to *fearsome* but most likely *fearful* people. As I look back on this experience, I am more and more aware of the importance of words—words we utter in prayer, as well as words we use with others. The Lord heard the words of my prayer and answered. My eccentric neighbor heard my words of acceptance and felt safe. My sister knows the words of my heart even when I cannot think of the words to say to thank her enough, and, of course, she laughs with me.

Thankfully, I enjoyed and learned that God's sense of humor, at least with me, was and is always a way of teaching me. After all, He has graced me with the ability to find something to laugh about in the most unlikely situations. Laughter is such a wonderful gift. It makes life so much brighter and leads us closer to the joy of the Lord.

> Commit your way to the Lord; Trust in him and he will act. (Psalm 37:5 RSV)

Prayer

Lord, I am so grateful for the gift of laughter, the gift of seeing something humorous in situations that are beyond the realm of understanding. Help me to try to bring a smile to all I meet, and when I am feeling blue, help me to wake up to the wonder of Your presence. May the joy You have given me flow into the minds of those who need lightheartedness and laughter. Thank You. Amen.

Travel Friend

God travels with me, and I need Him so.
When I'm lugging my luggage
He says, "Let it go."
When I'm merry and happy
He dances away.
He sings in my soul all through the day.
When I'm weary or lonely
He sees me through
And wipes my sad eyes as they mist up with dew.
He listens to me every day, every hour,
As He travels within me
Giving "grace power."
My traveling friend tabernacles within.
He fills up my heart
Till I can't help but grin.
God travels with me wherever I go.
He's my constant companion
And I need Him so.

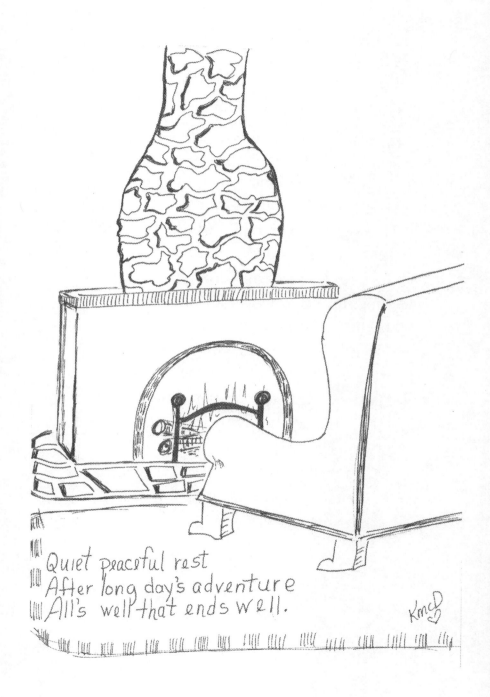

Quiet peaceful rest
After long day's adventure
All's well that ends well.

KmcD

The Chimney Monster

A cheerful heart is good medicine.

—Proverbs 17:22 (RSV)

This is a guaranteed-to-make-you-laugh story I wrote from my husband's perspective. He is a dear, jolly person, who delights me with his antics. Laughter should be a part of our spiritual walk, and Dick oozes with joy much of the time. So I am sharing this fun little story of one of his more humorous endeavors.

Although this event actually happened in our village, I took the author's liberty of placing him in the wilds. It makes for a nice atmosphere and fits him well. Enjoy.

~

There's something about getting older that spells *s-t-u-b-b-o-r-n*. If my son had just not given me "that look," or maybe if he'd not patiently told me that *he* would take care of it, I might not have gotten my hackles up. But, unfortunately, there was a strong hint in his expression, as well as in his voice, that maybe ***I*** was getting too old to be traipsing about on a snowy roof in the middle of January. That slight suggestion brought out the stubborn streak that lurks like a preying lion within me. I decided, even before his car inched slowly down the driveway, that I was going to do the job myself.

The chimney was my problem. It *was* too old (not like me), and it wasn't cooperating. Too much smoke was coming *into* my usually tranquil hunting cabin instead of going *out*. The darned thing needed cleaning, and snow or not, I was going to do it. After all, I'd come for a quiet weekend to get away from it all, and smoke was not part of my plan.

As soon as I saw my son take the last turn down my snowy, ice-covered gravel driveway, I figured I was safe. I gathered all the tools I needed, along with a ladder and a rope to tie around my waist just in case I slipped. Mind you, the rope had *nothing* to do with my age. It was only a precaution that a *wise* man would take.

I looked up and that culprit of a chimney stared down at me like a defiant child from its two-story perching place. I grumbled, wondering why I hadn't built a nice, simple log cabin instead of one that held the whole family. Then I gingerly climbed up the ladder to begin my job as chimney sweep.

I hummed to myself, thinking about Dick Van Dyke in the movie *Mary Poppins*. I had everything but his top hat. Balancing precariously on the roof peak, I began the tedious task of cleaning the chimney. I worked with a good deal of gusto, and as the chimney became cleaner and cleaner, I became blacker and blacker. Undaunted, I continued my task, changing position now and then to better my progress.

After some time, my curiosity got the best of me. I

wanted a better look into the chimney to see what kind of a job I was doing. I groped at my side to detach the flashlight lantern hooked to my belt. Wouldn't you know, my creosote-coated glove was slippery with soot, and for the life of me, I couldn't grab that flashlight with one hand. Since I was balancing myself and holding my cleaning tool with my other arm, I wasn't about to let go—I could see myself slowly sliding off the roof and hanging precariously in the air. So I put the glove up to my mouth to pull it off with my teeth. What an awful smell!

Then it happened. With my glove firmly grasped in my teeth, I pulled and then sneezed in rapid succession. The glove flew off my hand like the launch of a rocket and along with it my teeth—my tried-and-true, almost new teeth. I wobbled a second and then stood in stunned silence. My barren mouth gaped open. I watched my teeth soar into space. Then, like a fickle friend, they changed course. I swear they made a perfect right-angle turn and nose-dived down the chimney. In a kind of trance, I gazed unbelievingly down the black hole before me. I'd never believed in monsters, but right then I knew the chimney monster had attacked.

Oh well, I thought, *so much for a good fit.*

Now some people at that point might have reconsidered and possibly admitted that a younger man should finish the job. Not me! Was I going to admit defeat? I thought reasonably that there was nothing I could do about my teeth, and if I went down, I'd never come back up. The armchair by the fireplace would be too inviting, and I'd just sit there in front of the fire lamenting my teeth's demise. No way! I was going on with the job. No son of mine was going to have the last word.

Almost finished, I was startled by the voice of my neighbor, a hunter and trapper who was returning from checking his traplines. We usually checked on each other when we visited our digs in the winter. "Hey, Dick, didn't you pick the wrong month for that job, or has it taken you this long to figure out how to get down the chimney? Christmas was last month."

I chuckled. "Any Santa this dirty would surely not be invited back," I called. If only he knew that one of my finer parts had already made the trip.

He waved, laughing, and wandered back toward the woods. I guess he knew instinctively that this was not the time for a coffee break.

Finally, job finished, I climbed down. I was a toothless, old Santa Claus. I shed the sooty mess and soaked my clothes in a heavy soil remover. I was so tired as I stepped into the shower that for a moment I'd forgotten about my teeth. Finally, clean and just a little cocky about the success of my venture, I ambled toward the fireplace to investigate the fate of my expensive loss.

Behold! By some miracle, my teeth had made the whole journey and had even bounced neatly just outside the grate. They looked a bit like rotted bones, but at least they were alive and well. A few treatments of denture cleaner did the trick, and soon they rested again in my mouth. *Hmmm*, I thought, *not so bad after all*. I lit a fire in the fireplace, settled back in my comfortable old chair, and took a smug nap.

Next time I'll listen to my son. He might think he's made a point about my age, but I'll know better. It has nothing to do with my age as far as I can see, but I've had it with the chimney monster. Who knows what it'll be after next time, and aside from that, who wants all that soot? It's the clean life for me.

∼

Although laughter springs off the pages about Dick and his antics, this story also makes me aware of how God protected him in a precarious situation when he was not exactly using good sense. There is a lesson here too. It *is* okay to ask for help even if we are not *old*. Of course, I am sure that *none* of us has a problem with stubbornness. Ho-ho!

> You are my hiding place. You will protect me from trouble and surround me with songs of deliverance. (Psalm 32:7 NIV)

Prayer

Lord, thank You for blessing us with people who bring laughter as part of their ministry. Sometimes they can make us smile before they even say hello. Help us to be more aware of joy as well as silly things. After all, we are all Your children, and we need childlike delight to lighten our burdens. Give us, Lord, joyful hearts. Amen.

Laughter

Laughter singing through the air
So funny.
Tears fall like swirl of autumn leaves
Rivulets down smile-lined faces,
Belly-shaking joy
Of heart to heart and soul to soul.
What silly thing brought this on?
We look at each other
Just as
Unbidden giggles surface and off we go again,
Laughter pulling from some
Inside-shared-life-wonder.
Laughter
This gift that makes for friendship's life.

Questions to Contemplate or Discuss:

1. Share with a friend or a group, or write in your journal, a memorable laughter story.
2. Do you think God is there in simple things like fixing the plumbing or saving false teeth from destruction? Why or why not? Think about this and share with your group or journal.
3. In the first story, the author carries on a comfortable conversation with God. Share your thoughts about prayer as you understand it. Is your prayer a conversation throughout the day, or are you more apt to pray at specific times? Do you do both?
4. If you are a caregiver, share a time when you met with someone who, like Dick, was too stubborn to ask for help. What was the outcome?

Scripture Readings and Reflections:

Jeremiah 31:10–14
Psalm 33
1John 2:28–3:3

Activities:

1. Read a book that will make you laugh like *Anne of Green Gables* by L. M. Montgomery.
2. Watch one of those wonderful, classic comedy movies like *Bringing Up Baby*, *Arsenic and Old Lace*, or *Harvey*.

Personal Reflections

Surprise student-gift

World of wonders to learn but

Who is teaching who?

Part 3

Stories of Perseverance

The Report

> Better is the end of a thing than its beginning, and the patient in spirit is better than the proud in spirit.
>
> —Ecclesiastes 7:8 (RSV)

Everything was running like clockwork in my fifth grade classroom on that crisp November day. All my cooperative student groups had accepted their responsibilities and settled in, and they were beginning to work with efficiency. It was one of those rare years when everyone seemed well matched, and I was feeling positive, peaceful, and perhaps a little smug about my good luck. Then, with a knock on the door and a turn of the knob, my class, my focus, and my life was put into flux.

My principal led a girl into my room. She was an awkward little sight. Her hair hung in thin tresses, and her skin looked abrasive, almost as if someone had rubbed it with sandpaper. Her expression was like a painting of one whose endless searching had etched itself on olive skin. Her deeply sad blue eyes appeared to be those of a very young yet very old person all stirred up into one frightened girl. I'll call her Chenille.

I introduced her to the class and then managed to seat and engage her quickly with a worksheet. I begged her pardon and went into the hall to talk to her waiting mother, who nervously looked from me to the principal and stated her list of Chenille's needs. First she needed counseling, as they had moved from place to place for the past two years. Her father had abandoned them, and there had been several deaths in the family in a short span of time; thus, Chenille was hesitant to make friends for fear of loss. I stifled a sigh as a tiny cloud formed in the atmosphere of my mind. It looked like there might be a storm ahead. I hoped I was ready for it.

By the end of the week, I had to admit that my first impression seemed mild. Chenille's letter formation was, at the most, preprimary. I couldn't interpret what she was trying to write, let alone read it. Her oral reading was halting, and she spent the greater part of her math period looking around. During class discussions, she added rather bizarre comments. Instead of accepting God's will on the spot, I prayed for patience and thought, *How can this be happening to me right now?*

I studied her records and examples of her work and convinced myself that there was no way for me to handle this child effectively. Doing what I call my Moses-and-Gideon-avoidance protocol, I made my way to the special education office, convincing myself there was surely a better placement for this child. My friends there were surprised, as I usually enjoyed students who were challenging. They gave me a sheaf of forms to fill out and sent me on my way.

After many years of walking with the Lord, you would think that I would know enough to just say yes. However, He once again had to use the sledgehammer treatment on my strong-willed brain. In any case, I resisted and put up my protective wall. I was *not* going to like this, and that was that. (How foolhardy are the Jonahs in this world.) I rationalized that there could be no earthly good in putting this girl into a class where she would be misplaced and subject to ridicule. How could I possibly help *another* child with so many in the class already needing extra help? I was going to resist, or so I thought.

Despite my stubborn resolve, I still made the normal effort to try to help Chenille adjust to my class. However, it was not easy because every strategy I tried, failed. I was exhausting my little bag of tricks. I signed her up for any available extra help, but even in a small group, she had a difficult time. The remedial teachers were floored by both her defensive attitude and her outlandish comments and stories. Determining what was fact and what was fiction made her a true enigma.

During those first few weeks, we had several special speakers visit our grade level. Chenille had a story of some curious incident that fit in with each guest's topic. During Fire Prevention Week, for instance, she told of the serious fire she had lived through. When the state trooper who taught the DARE program (a drug and alcohol prevention program for middle-school children) spoke, she not only told about a drug bust that she had witnessed but also described a murder that had supposedly occurred right before her eyes. You name it, she had had a personal experience with it.

With follow-up checking on her many escapades, it didn't take long to realize that this child had a very vivid imagination. She was a convincing storyteller. The students' reactions ranged from "Here we go again" to "Wow!" I was always trying to tone things down and nip her stories in the bud.

Trying to help her assimilate was further complicated by her bizarre and highly inappropriate choice of dress. At first I thought that she had nothing else to wear, but as I got to know her, I realized that her tastes were as eccentric as her personality. She had no idea about how to dress and was physically mature for a fifth grader, which compounded the problem. Her personal hygiene was also poor. Her organizational skills were almost hopeless, and *needy* became a much too simple word to describe her.

I assume that most teachers, at some time or another, have had a throw-up-your-hands type of student. Before getting to that point, I prayed again and again for insight. My heart began to ache for her while my spirit softened. There were no two ways about it: she was a troubled child and needed love. The job of teacher requires selfless ingenuity and the ability to meet a challenge. I'd just forgotten that for a while. In all truthfulness, she did such peculiar things that it made me laugh in my heart.

When I finished my paperwork for special needs testing, I met with her mother to convince her that this would be a positive step to help her daughter. Mom's demeanor when she arrived was defensive, but when I explained that I wanted her permission to test Chenille to see if there was any type of learning disability, the mother looked surprised. She told me that she had begged for some kind of testing at the last school and had been refused. She knew there was something amiss but did not know what to do or how to get help. She readily signed the papers and was relieved to know that there might be help for her daughter, as well as herself.

Depending on the year and the number of students who need testing, it can take some time before the actual testing occurs. It was getting harder to wait. Chenille needed help, and I needed to know what I was dealing with.

One morning, I went in tears to see my principal. I shared my frustration with seeing one idea after another fail and asked if he could intervene to push up the date for Chenille's testing. He agreed to see what could be done and encouraged me, letting me know that my efforts had not gone unnoticed.

Because all things work together for good, each succeeding event seemed to show me that prayer was being answered. Chenille, adroit with words, walked into the principal's office herself the very next day. She sat down with him and proceeded to cry. She told him that she really didn't know what to do. She wanted to do the work, but she couldn't. She told him how much she wanted to please me. "I really need help," she cried. If I had not been convincing enough, Chenille put an exclamation point on my plea. My boss came up to share this incident and assured me that he was in our corner. Chenille would be placed first on the list to be tested.

In my class I was fortunate to have a lovely, insightful girl who had what I call a "seeing heart." I will call her Hope. At the beginning of the year, I had given my class writing logs. Each day they wrote their thoughts and concerns to me, and I wrote back to them. Hope wrote me a note about Chenille. Through her gift of words, I could see her classmate's needs from a different perspective. This helped me to understand my own frustration and see some new possibilities. Hope readily took on the job of helping Chenille in the classroom. Ironically, all of these things happened within a two-day window. It was a turning point.

I continued to try new strategies. I'd enrolled Chenille in an after-school small group program for children who had trouble getting their work done. Unfortunately, the program was not effective for my problem child. The teacher who oversaw it was totally flummoxed as she tried to meet Chenille's needs. My gal distracted everyone there and needed too much one-on-one help.

While waiting for testing, I documented events and my concerns. When I talked to Chenille, she used surprisingly good vocabulary and was convincing. She was intelligent. I recognized the symptoms of attention deficit disorder (ADD), in which a student cannot pay attention very long or stay to task. In addition, her restlessness indicated hyperactivity. She was most likely right brained (a person who operates mainly on the right or creative side of the brain). This would explain her stories, imagination, and basic disorganization. Because she moved from school to school, she apparently had not assimilated basic skills. She had a low opinion of herself due to a pattern of failure. Her home life appeared to be chaotic too, which only exacerbated her problems. But I had an ace in the hole. She loved me and wanted to please me; therefore, I would keep trying. If I could manage to work with her alone while we waited for testing, perhaps I could get a head start.

Because of the needs of other kids in the class, I knew I could not fit this extra service in during the regular day. I talked to her mom about helping Chenille after school, and she gratefully agreed. Chenille was a walker, not affected by a bus schedule, so we quickly embarked on after-school sessions.

When I started, I went one step at a time, finding the best way to make the sessions productive and interesting. I decided to start with her reading homework, which included a fifteen-minute reading time followed by a short written summary. She had *never* completed that assignment, and I knew reading would tell me much about her. In a quiet setting without distractions, I could test her comprehension as well as her ability to concentrate. Hopefully, I would get a glimpse into her thought patterns and see what she valued.

At first, Chenille tried to get out of staying with me after school. But I stuck to my guns. When she knew I meant business, she settled down. We fell into a good pattern. Reading came first. I gave her time to read alone. Then I sat down and read with her as soon as she appeared distracted. Interestingly enough, she had a fine grasp of the content and even an insightful one. As in most aspects of learning, the more you do, the better you become. She gradually increased her reading time and gained confidence.

On the other hand, unlike reading, her progress in written expression was a serious problem. Getting ideas down on paper was beyond her capacity despite the fact that she vocalized them beautifully. So she dictated her reading summary to me. When she saw it written down and realized how good her ideas were, she was delighted and made it her goal to come up with a unique, often profound insight each day. She fell easily into thinking up a good summary. It was rewarding to be part of this development.

One day in class, we'd studied the types of conflict presented in realistic fiction. After school, when I was writing her dictation, she informed me that there were several types of conflict in the book she was presently reading. As she began to list them, it was obvious she really understood the lesson I had taught that morning. What a joy!

During class, I had to continually remind her to stay on task. I joked with her about forgetting what she was doing on the way to the pencil sharpener. Eventually, the committee on the handicapped tested Chenille. Just as I thought, she was so ADHD that she almost scored off the charts. The committee confirmed my analysis that she was learning disabled in written expression as well as in spelling. Her scores showed that her basic intelligence was high and that with the proper guidance, she could excel. The bad news was the special education classes that year were so full that they would not have room for her until fall. So I continued the same format, which was working well, and we added an assigned remedial writing teacher who could take dictation.

In May, I assigned a US state research project. Each child in the class was responsible for researching information about their state, coming up with interesting visual aids, and finally presenting the material to the class. I was concerned about Chenille getting this project done since I could foresee many hours of working with her streaming out in front of me like a river. *One step at a time*, I thought.

Through the weeks, we read the material and discussed it together. I took notes for her. She began to make inferences, and I was amazed at her reasoning and understanding of the material. I wondered how she might retain the information and be able to systematically present it to the class.

During this time, we developed a fine student-teacher type of friendship. Her sense of humor was priceless, and her loyalty was strong, especially for someone who had little nurturing at home. I, in turn, was learning a new type of patience. I enjoyed her blooming interest in reading and the small improvements in her writing, still dictated but developing. Because she trusted me, I was able to help her with hygiene and her dress code. She was growing. I was too.

The last two days before Chenille had to give the report, we worked diligently to finish up and put all of her research in order. We devised a plan for her oral presentation. She grudgingly practiced using simple notes, the overhead projector, and other visuals. She was "taxed to the max" when she went home. I don't know about Chenille, but I had trouble sleeping the night before her talk. It felt like my own child was venturing into a new endeavor.

∼

The time had come. Chenille was setting up her work, and I could see how shaky she was feeling. I took her out of the room for a few minutes. We walked to the window at the end of the hall, and I said a prayer for her. She looked at me with determination and assured me that she was going to be the teacher of the day.

What happened next was nothing short of miraculous. Chenille presented a most interesting and well-developed report about her state, Louisiana. She not only gave the basic information that we had practiced but also interspersed it with material she had found interesting along the way. The kids were rapt.

Because of her ADHD, there were a few times when she almost got off task, but when I gently reminded her, she quickly returned to her report. I sat in absolute amazement. A wonderful feeling of thanksgiving and awe swept through me—a special touch from the Lord.

But yet to come was the most amazing part of the whole report. She gave a biographical sketch of jazz great Louis Armstrong. It was based on a book she had read on her own. We hadn't had time to work on it together. Now, here she stood relating the story of a young man who had struggled to make it in life. Her understanding of the book was awesome as was her presentation. This man had touched her life, and she was touching mine with the knowledge that all those nights after school had been worth it.

When she finished, my class gave many compliments to their rather eccentric classmate—a girl they had never really accepted. You could see her self-worth growing, and I was thrilled.

At gym time I went to tell the principal. He was a dear man, and his eyes filled with tears as he remembered the day she had burst into his office, despondent. As I left the office, he was on his way to the gym to compliment her. After school that night, Chenille floated into the room and we rejoiced together.

That year quickly ended. The teachers on my floor stopped by and told me I could not put in that much after-school time on students every year. (In addition to Chenille, several other students had stayed after school for help.) I knew that. I was tired. I was behind. I was whipped. I also knew that I had seen so much growth in Chenille and that the Lord had taught me great lessons during the entire time. I knew she was grateful and that I had made a small difference in her fragile life.

I have seen Chenille off and on since those days, and it is always delightful. She is one of the many reasons that I chose to teach. In helping her grow, I grew. In helping her see her potential, I learned more about my own. In modeling for her, I may have sown a seed of success in her life and set it on the right track. But the best thing about the whole experience is that I don't take the credit. Teaching is a *gift*, and when we do it right, it is only giving back the glory to the Gift Giver.

It is not hard to see God's little miracles in this story. Acceptance, determination, courage, and a butterfly taking wing are all rolled up into this classroom story from life. What a privilege to have been a part of it all.

> Enter His gates with thanksgiving and His courts with praise! Give thanks to Him; bless His name. (Psalm100:4 RSV)

Prayer

Dear Lord, thank You for Your patience with us as we try to take over situations and close our ears to Your calling. You wait while we make ourselves miserable trying to do things ourselves. Defeated, we finally realize what You have been telling us all of the time: "Just trust Me. I placed you in this situation because I knew you could handle it."

Lord, many of us are so much like Jonah. Again and again You deal lovingly with us as we are such slow learners. Help us, Lord, to learn, accept, and go to our Nineveh immediately with trusting hearts. Amen.

Gift

What is this gift you've given me—
My heart to lend and eyes to see?
A lovely challenge offered here
A needy lass so full of fear.
I, foolish, try to run away,
But You, persistent, and order, "Stay."
Resigned, I finally see the light.
I say, "I will," and cease my flight.
I take her proffered hand in mine
And mold myself to Your design.
Grace abounds more and more
As this fledgling child begins to soar.

A Gentle Gift

> He is like a tree planted by streams of water that yields its fruit in due season, and its leaf does not wither. In all that he does, he prospers.
>
> —Psalm 1:3 (RSV)

I was casually gleaning my writing ideas when I came across a story called "Old Trucks." It is a story written by one of my former pupils that I have kept so long it is discolored. It gave me great joy to reread it and remember a young student I'll call Shane. He was one of those dear children who pass through a teacher's life and leave an imprint on the heart. What a joy, what a challenge, and oh how much I learned while working with this fine young man. I felt my heart flutter with the memory and knew I must share his story.

The small Christian school where I taught at that time was a family affair. Everyone knew each other, and one child's problems were the concern of all—teacher, student, and parents. The weaker students were watched over by all the members of the class and for the most part were protected from ridicule and bullying. Thus, the needy were essentially wrapped up in a warm blanket of love.

Sometimes, however, love needs to be tough. Sometimes love needs to wake up a sleeping problem and send it screaming into reality. So it was with Shane, who arrived in my classroom awkward, shy, and smiling.

My preference as a teacher was to meet my students, get to know them, and make my own observations before reviewing their records. In that way, I could start with a clean slate while honing my teacher sensitivities. Shane was interesting from the first moment. He had a heart of gold and a gentle spirit. He jumped at the chance to be helpful and gave his best effort to whatever was asked of him.

The class cutup was his best friend. Let's call him Dave. For the most part, the sensible students stayed away from Dave, as he was generally in trouble for some reason or another. Not Shane. He sensed that his friend needed someone in his corner. Shane was right there, trying to fill the gap of love, and somewhat like Jonathan (King David's friend), he gave faithful and stern allegiance to his wayward pal. In my notes from that year, I recorded one of Shane's right-on statements chiding Dave: "If you keep doing things like that, Dave, I'll sure think your brain's no bigger than a pea." I laughed inside as Dave responded with chagrin, promising to try harder to do the right thing.

It wasn't long before I noted how Shane struggled himself. He was disorganized, always losing things, and was often lost in the concepts taught in subjects like social studies and science. He did adequate work if it was given in small chunks because his attention span was short. It took time for him to process information, but with patience he usually came up with the right answer. His ideas were wonderful, but he had little understanding of the basics of grammar so it was often hard to read his work.

I began to think that he had slipped through the cracks as he advanced through the years of school. Probably he did enough to get by but never reached his potential. I surmised that he might need some one-on-one help. So I read his records and talked to other teachers who had had him in class. I discovered that he started kindergarten with few cognitive skills and minimal readiness. His birth mother was an alcoholic and had left when he was tiny. He had been tested by the school psychologist but, oddly, never classified. With this information, I applied my own teaching ideas and continued to observe.

One of the most interesting problems he exhibited involved spatial relationships. I feel that students who have an artistic gift should be encouraged to learn using their talent. So if a unit invited visual learning, I let them use the blackboard or poster-sized newsprint to display their gifts. Thus, our classroom would often be adorned with drawings to accompany units on such topics as ancient Egypt, scientific classification, and Japanese haiku. In like manner, the analytical pupils did hands-on projects in cooperative groups. Because Shane liked to draw, the drawing component seemed the perfect outlet for him.

I was excited the first time that I gave Shane colored chalk and his own blackboard section. It was a science project. He chose a picture to draw and went happily to the blackboard to show off his gift. It was a large space, but he started drawing a very small picture. I went up to help him see the dimensions of the drawing and attempted to orient him to the space involved. Still, although he drew a beautiful picture, it took up less than a quarter of the space. I had not run into this problem before, as he truly saw nothing unusual about his work. I needed to do some research.

As I read and looked at Shane's learning style, I began to suspect fetal alcohol syndrome (FAS), a condition where the fetus of an alcoholic ingests some alcohol while in the womb. The various parts of the brain are affected, as the fetus cannot pass all of the alcohol through his or her developing liver. This syndrome is often overlooked unless the doctors or other professionals know the habits of the mother. I wondered about Shane. I was especially concerned for him because he would enter junior high in a large school the next year. I felt it imperative that he receive an appropriate IEP (Individualized Education Program), as the transition for this dear young man would be overwhelming.

I investigated and found a doctor in a nearby city who specialized in birth defects and diagnosing learning problems. Then I met with his family. Shane's parents were wonderful. His father, a quiet man, and his friendly, concerned stepmother, along with his grandmother, were all truly in Shane's corner. (Their love and patience probably accounted for his own kindness, as I never heard him say an unkind word or do an unkind deed.) What a relief! They were more than open to getting to the bottom of his problems and had a high interest in helping Shane. They were baffled after trying many ways to help him.

We set up an appointment with the doctor, and my supposition was verified. The doctor provided wise advice. Shane was classified as a potentially high achiever who, with the use of proper learning tools, would be successful. It was a joy to know not only that would he be protected but also that he would have some expert direction for use in the classroom. His family and I were ready to truly help him.

One of the key elements of progress for Shane was to assign small chunks of work that he could complete without feeling overwhelmed. One of my fondest memories was choosing the topic "trucks" for a writing project. If he would write a story, I promised to help him with the sentence structure and grammar. Now there were two things that motivated this young man: nature and trucks. He wrote about trucks, worked on trucks with his father, and dreamed of having his own truck to restore. So he was in his element and gleefully went to work. He was so proud of himself when he turned in his finished copy.

Here is a sample from his best story called "Old Trucks":

> I like to take a walk and find old rusty trucks in the weeds. Old trucks smell moldy and dusty. I wonder if old trucks will be around when I grow up ... Sometimes it takes a year to restore an old truck. The motor gets stuck and parts rust and join together. First you take it apart and try to put all the parts together ...

Dad and I paint the engine. We put the cab on, and the fenders and the bed on the back ...

We like to name our old trucks. One we named "Gunther" ... sometimes we put Gunther in parades.

This is pretty good writing for a young man, who if faced with a standard sixth grade composition topic would have frozen and looked like he had just entered *The Twilight Zone*. He actually asked if he could read his story to the class. Needless to say, I used his two interests to reach him in many ways.

I can still see my gawky, preadolescent young man with his glasses hanging a little off kilter and his big smile. His heart was even bigger. He had such a good sense of humor and was so accepting of who he was. I can still see him working on projects like a medieval castle and hear him making simple statements of truth to his classmates.

Occasionally I see him today. What a handsome guy he has turned out to be! He finished his education with the proper help, and he did get that old rusty truck to work on when he was older. Better yet, I bet you'll never guess what he does for a living—he drives a large delivery truck. He is still a smiling delight and looks as happy as a bear that has just found a honeycomb.

To me, Shane's story is another of God's little miracles. God allowed me to use my background in Al-Anon, a support group for families of alcoholics (see *Simpler Times:*

Reflections on Women's Friendship), to realize that he might have a particular problem. God gave his family the wisdom to go that extra step to determine what was causing his learning problems and discover how to deal with them. Because of their love for Shane, they gave him the gift of testing in hopes of providing a good, safe future for their boy. The right doctor was available for proper testing, giving direction to both the family and me. Most of all, this young man had a spirit that never gave up and was finally given the educational tools he needed to succeed. He went on to that larger school in safe hands, and everything worked together to give one young man the chance to reach his potential.

I guess I will make a copy of that tattered old story to put in my teaching scrapbook. When I see him again, I will give him his copy and share this story with him. I wonder if he will remember.

> For you have delivered my soul from death, my eyes from tears, and my feet from stumbling; I will walk before the Lord in the land of the living. (Psalm116:8RSV)

Prayer

Dear Lord, thank You for the gift of awareness, for seeing the beauty in each person as well as the need that may be lingering there. Thank You for placing special people in our lives that nurture us with their simplicity and love. Thank You for hearts that see beyond the surface and, with wisdom, dare to go the extra mile to help another on their way. Help us to see others with Your eyes and love others with Your heart. In the name of Jesus, Amen.

Challenge

Oh, that old rusty truck sitting there among the weeds
Almost invisible it blends in,
Playing hide and seek with some lost opponent
Who quit the game long before done.
Stopped looking
Stopped caring
Until a curious hand moved aside the bush
Near that hidden memory
And found to his delight a treasure
to pull out and save.
Start loving
Start changing
From cold, damp forgotten place
To scrub, to paint, to polish.
New life born as little by little
Skillful hands bring new life into old death.

Questions to Contemplate or Discuss:

Take a little time to think about the similarities and differences between Chenille and Shane. What can you learn from each of them? Can one or both of their stories help you to see someone in your life a little differently?

1. Teachers have a great impact on our lives. Think about a teacher who was especially helpful to you, and share your story in your group or journal.
2. If you are a teacher or caregiver, share a time when you felt the Lord asked you to accomplish an almost impossible task.

Scripture Readings and Reflections:

Psalm 23
Matthew 18:10–14
John 10:1–18

Activities:

1. If possible, find that teacher who had an impact on your life and contact him or her with a card or a note, letting that person know how much he or she meant to you and why. Send an old and a new picture so he or she will remember you. Teachers love their old students to remember them.
2. A book to read: the James Hilton classic, *Goodbye Mr. Chips*.

Personal Reflections:

Majestic Maple
Lovely green summer hues
Red orange fall song

Part 4

Stories of Joy

The Miracle Maple

There shall come forth a shoot from the stump of Jesse, and a branch shall grow out of his roots.

—Isaiah11:1 (RSV)

It was a fine spring morning. My son, Justin, home from college, was enjoying some quality time with his stepdad. They'd talked the night before about getting a tree to plant in the front yard. I'd suggested going to the nearby nursery, but they just looked at me incredulously. That suggestion presented no challenge whatsoever to their masculinity. After all, my husband's friend, Ed, owned a tree farm.

"He'll let us have a tree for free. He's always offering. We just have to dig it up," my husband, Dick, stated with assured reason.

It was easy to see that the thought of wandering through Ed's tree farm excited their imaginations, so the plan was finalized. They got up at the crack of dawn to dig a hole for their tree.

I went off to work, waving goodbye, as the two tree hunters gathered gear for their excursion. They were all smiles. Little did I know the surprise that would await me when I returned home.

Graciously, Ed offered them any tree they would like. We love sugar maples and wanted a shade tree, so it was an easy choice for Dick and Justin. Pensively, Dick began to calculate his age against the time it would take to grow a shade tree. My husband, with the agreement of my adventurous son, decided, "Why wait? Let's get some shade now!" So instead of picking a nice strong sapling or even a nursery-size starter tree, they chose to dig up a young tree that was twenty-five feet tall! Yes, I did say twenty-five feet tall.

They labored all day long as blissful comrades. The sweat and aching muscles became a challenge not to be hindered by common sense. Then, work done, they loaded their oversized booty precariously onto the *too small* pickup truck and readied themselves for their trip home. As the truck lumbered out of the woods, Ed shook his head in disbelief.

It was a slow trip with many stops as Dick and Justin maneuvered their cargo along the road home. Unfortunately, one of the main limbs was sacrificed in the process, but eventually the truck showed up on our street and teetered into the driveway. By this time, most of the men in our neighborhood were home from work and wandered over to our house, curious to see what was going on.

Needless to say, Justin and Dick puffed up with manly pride and told the story of their day's adventure. Soon the neighbors offered other big-fish stories. Laughter and gaiety filled the neighborhood.

Of course, the hole Justin and Dick had dug was a bit small for this mammoth prize. It was time for the neighborhood men to join in on the action, along with one of Justin's pals who had dropped by. So the fun of making the proper-sized home for this beleaguered tree began. Like a new baby, our new tree had bonded with the neighborhood.

About this time, I rounded the corner on my way home from work. What was going on? The whole neighborhood was in my front yard. Digging, balancing, pushing, and pulling, the slow process was completed with much laughter and many remember-the-time stories mingled into the work. Finally, the poor tree was in place and tied on all sides with support stakes. The workers and the tree looked more than a bit weary. However, no matter how tired that specimen looked, it was a proud testament to determination as well as a true monument to madness.

During the next few weeks, we all took turns talking to the tree, saying prayers for it, and using remedies to heal its wounds. Finally it responded and grew a few new branches to let us know it was going to make it. We spent several years continuing to work on the wound it received in transport, but it survived. Eventually, it showed its pride by sporting its first bird's nest in the spring and a myriad of color in the fall. We took down the stakes, and it stood its ground.

Then, one fall day, my husband picked me up at the airport. I had returned from a trip to Italy with my daughter, so I was tired and excited. I spent the long ride home telling him the adventures Missy and I had had together. As we got closer to home, Dick wore a serious look on his face. I tried to figure out what was wrong, and as we turned the corner of our block, I immediately knew what was bothering him. There, lying on the ground was our lovely tree. The night before a mighty windstorm had blown it down. Dick, thoughtful person that he is, didn't want me to know about it until I'd shared my exciting Italian adventure.

Over the next few days, neighbors came to pay their respects—after all, it was a neighborhood icon. Dick and I sadly cleared away the branches. In the spring, we tore away the protective mulch and worked the ground around the trunk. Always hopeful, we ringed it with flowers, and I placed a pretty decoration on top of the trunk. Maybe, just maybe, a sapling would sprout from the roots.

A couple of months later, Justin, who had come home for a few days from his new home in South Carolina, was preparing to leave when we happened to look at the stump. There, a small red and green sapling smiled up at us. Like children finding a treasure, we all rejoiced. What a wonder it was that the three of us found this new life surprise together.

As soon as we returned from taking Justin to the airport, we put protection around the tree so little feet and animal wanderers would not hinder its growth. Then I, the romantic in the family, put up a wrought iron shepherd's crook with a tinkling wind chime to give the little tree music. What a delightful miracle! In our eyes, this was definitely a gift from God, and of course, we felt the Shepherd was at work on our tree.

Now the tree stands about thirty feet tall. It is strong and healthy. I rejoice every time I look at it and smile at its endurance. The stump from which it grew has settled into the ground and rests under the mulch. Each time we have a storm, I still say a little prayer for our miracle maple's safety.

Like most things that happen in my life, I usually try to see some spiritual connection—some message that God might be whispering to me if I would just listen. So this spirited little tree has given me hope in other ways too. It serves as a reminder that when I fall from my wounds, there is always a nurturing, loving God who helps me heal. The tree's determined growth encourages me to press on and keep growing. The branches reach upward as if in prayer and remind me to honor my Maker. Just as He watches over our miracle tree, He watches over my life and guides me onward and upward toward my final destination. The miracle maple stands as a kind of testament to the care of a gracious God.

> The Lord is my strength and my shield; my heart trusts in Him and I am helped. My heart leaps for joy and I will give thanks to Him in song. (Psalm 28:7 NIV)

Prayer

Lord, trees are so fascinating—so many kinds, so many sizes, so many shapes. I wonder, do You laugh with joy at each odd knot or unusual branch like I do?

Trees have so much to teach about life. Their roots hold them down like Your grace holds us. Inside they show the growth of each year, drought years and plentiful years. Isn't that so like our walk with You? Their bruises stay with them and become part of their story, often turning into beautiful and unique shapes. They change with the seasons as we do with our lives. Their branches reach up like our hands in prayer, and leaves rustle, singing in the wind. Little animals safely hide in their leaf cover like we hide in the shelter of Your wings.

Trees—Lord, what a testament to Your creative imagining. Help us to look at nature in new ways and contemplate the gifts You offer there. Let us be appreciative and thankful. Amen.

Tree Treasure

Marvelous maple miracle
You stand so stately stretching toward the sky.
Who would ever know you sprang
From some fallen tree's trunk
Now hidden in the earth below.
Good from brokenness …
Life from hope amidst sorrow …
Song-singing-leaves in spring sunrise
As wind wafts through.
Birds join in as branches sway
Hymn of thanksgiving
For chance at life renewed.

A Small Miracle

She seeks wool and flax and works with willing hands.

—Proverbs 31:13 (RSV)

She opens her hand to the poor and reaches out her hands to the needy.

—Proverbs 31:20 (RSV)

My mother, Ella, was a woman of faith. Quiet, with a refined English demeanor, she went about her business with determination. Then regularly at three in the afternoon, she paused and made green tea with cream and added a small crumpet—truly English. In the summers, it was not unusual to find my mother under our quiet little orchard of cherry trees enjoying this ritual in the shade, basking in the summer breezes. I looked forward to sharing those times with her while her grandkids played nearby.

    A somewhat solitary person, she delighted in her rock garden and houseplants, and perused Dickens and Shakespeare with classical aplomb, enchanted by their subtle humor. I remember her resolve that before she died she was going to finish *Bleak*

House, one of Dickens's lengthiest offerings. (She is also the only person I know who read the dictionary from beginning to end.) Although she preferred the quiet life, she was a natural caregiver, especially when dealing with the infirm and the dying.

One summer afternoon, I joined Mother for tea. She seemed excited and patiently waited for me to sit down. I could tell she was ready to tell me something special. As I quickly settled into a lawn chair, her eyes filled with tears and she said, "Kathy, I think I've experienced a small miracle!" Ella was hardly the fanciful type, so if she said it was a miracle, it probably was. I sat in anticipation, ready to hear her story.

It was the afghan, the one she had so lovingly made when my sisters and I were young. Making it was a labor of love and also a battle of will as she wasn't a craft enthusiast. She decided one day that an afghan was something every family needed, something to pass down from generation to generation. Her vocation as wife and mother suddenly depended on making this symbolic family gift.

Patiently she learned to crochet that first granny square. She worked one square at a time over a period of years. I can remember her little basket of yarn and the crochet hook sitting near her chair.

Money did not come easy, and a skein of yarn was like a golden nugget to our struggling farm family. She wasted not one strand of the yarn, gathering scraps here and there. Finally her family heirloom was finished and was proudly displayed for many years on the back of our living room couch. The love of a mother's heart was sewn into every piece.

Mother treated that afghan with special care. It was all wool and needed minimal but careful hand-washing. After many years of washings, she began to be more protective of the aging blanket. She began to put it out on the line for airing and let the breezes blow softly through its mature strands.

So, to get on with her story, on a sunny summer Sunday after church, she took her treasure out, hung it gently on the line, and walked up the road to visit my invalid aunt, Annie. As Mother shared her story, I was pleased because she rarely mentioned her many visits to family members who needed simple comforts like physical care or just someone to talk to. This Sunday, Annie was especially happy to have company and lit up like a lamp.

Mother picked a bouquet of pansies and brought them in with her to delight Annie, whose pansy garden had been her pride and joy. Now homebound and in the early stages of Alzheimer's disease, the dear soul was often alone. Her parents had died, and her sister was quite busy. Mother settled comfortably into a cozy chair and prepared to be there out of love for Annie. Fortunately, Annie was quite lucid that day and relished someone to talk to.

Suddenly, there was a distant roll of thunder, and like an ornery child who did not get his or her way, the sky darkened and lightning zipped through the clouds. In no time at all, rain was beating down on the sighing ground. The wind was blowing, and a typical summer storm was in full-fledged progress.

Poor Ella's stomach lurched, and her head spun a little. "Oh Lord, my poor old afghan!" she breathed out in a simple, silent prayer. "Can my old treasure withstand this deluge?"

Annie continued chatting happily for another hour, unaware of the concern that filled Mother's eyes. Nonetheless, she stayed and continued to be a sacrament to this sweet, lonely lady.

The rain had stopped by the time Mother made her way home. The trees dripped, and the road was wet with puddles. She trudged down the stone walk into our backyard and saw that everything around her was drenched. She looked ahead at the clothesline and gasped. Uttering a prayer of thanks, she hurried toward the clothesline where her treasure hung in one piece. Her muddy feet made prints on dry stone. She bent over in disbelief and touched the grass. It was dry. She hurried the few steps left and felt her work of love; it too was dry. Not a drop of water had fallen all around the clothesline, and the afghan gently moving in the breeze seemed to smile at her. It surely was a small miracle.

Mother was so animated as she ended her tale that I could feel her swelling heart. It was so profound and yet so simple a lesson. While Mother had been doing the Lord's work, He was doing a special work for her. How like our God who gives us surprise after surprise.

I have that wonderful old afghan now. It is none the worse for wear, as some might say, but it will always be one of my most valued treasures. Mother valued it, our family valued it, and God valued it too.

> The heavens declare the glory of God; the skies proclaim the work of his hands. (Psalm 19:1 NIV)

Prayer

Lord, thank You, thank You, thank You for your little miracles—Your special ways of letting us know You are there. Give us faith to believe that there really are no coincidences, and that even in this vast universe, You are interested in each of us. It boggles our minds when we try to grasp Your omnipotence. Yet You reassure us over and over again that You care. Lord, open our eyes so we will ever see Your presence around us. Amen.

Needlework

Over, under, up, and down,
Fingers moving clasped around
a simple crochet hook.
Stitch, stitch, stitch…a muted sound
As yarn is woven neatly wound
With simple crochet hook.
The lovely colors blend in true.
The balls of yarn, they wink at you
And work with crochet hook.
Yarns come to life in every hue.
"Just watch and see what we can do!"
They wind on crochet hook.
The working hands, they stop to rest,
A finished product at its best:
The art of crochet hook.
The afghan work now finally done,
A gift of lovely art-homespun.
Now rests the crochet hook.

Questions to Contemplate or Discuss:

1. In "The Miracle Maple," Justin and his dad created a father-son memory. Remember and share a story about an event you enjoyed with your parent or child.
2. In "The Little Miracle," the author's mother shared an intimate slice-of-life story. There was an unspoken confidence between Ella and her daughter of acceptance and understanding. Do you have a confidant with whom you can share a deep spiritual experience? If not, what holds you back?
3. Share a story that you consider a miracle in your life or the life of someone you know.

Scripture Readings and Reflections:

Matthew 13:31–32
Psalm 1
1Kings 17:7–16

Activities:

1. Plant a tree with someone in your family; name and nurture it together.
2. If you knit or crochet, make a prayer shawl for someone who is older or infirm. When you take it to him or her, read the story of "The Little Miracle" to that person.

Personal Reflections:

Part 5

Stories of Awareness

Boxes of Memories

I will bless the Lord at all times; His praise will always be on my lips.

—Psalm 34:1(NIV)

I love boxes—wooden or tin ones, elegantly decorated or velvety soft ones. If it has character and it is a box, I am drawn to it. I have a wide assortment sitting here and there in my house filled with all kinds of wonderful things like letters and cards, my grandchildren's artwork, my scrapbooking supplies, and so forth. If I can't use a particularly lovely box that I find, I immediately think of someone else who might love it. I imagine the delight the gift will bring to a friend or family member.

I even like waiting-to-be-fixed boxes found at estate and garage sales. Sometimes they just need to be cleaned up, polished, or repaired. To me, a mystery lies in each one, a story lurking under each lid. Occasionally an old box will open up to a cache of old costume jewelry, curious shaped buttons, or some such surprise. Like a child, I grab up the booty and pay for the best find of the day.

Being the introspective type, I looked back over my life to solve the mystery of my long romance with boxes. Why do they seem to call to me? Suddenly, larger than life, I remembered my grandmother.

Grandma, coming from the old country as they called Europe in her day, had lived modestly and worked hard all of her life. By the time I came along, she had seen a depression and two world wars, raised nine children, and shrunk to a tiny lady whose hands alone told stories of years of hard work. She still was a whirlwind of energy. Her kitchen was a busy place where cooking and canning, laundry and ironing provided constant exercise.

Despite all the activity, she always had time for her grandchildren. Not only did she have time for us, but she also made each of us feel like we were *the* most special one. I can still see my little grandmother sitting beside me on the wooden bench by her flower garden. I can almost feel her gnarled, wrinkled hand holding mine. I see her hair in its pulled-back bun and her simple housedress covered with a clean though well-stained apron. I see thick stockings hiding her legs and her wonderfully old-fashioned black tie-up shoes that seemed to be molded to her feet. That resting place was her refueling station, a stop between jobs before she'd be busy again. She was a wiry wisp of a thing in her elderly years.

Sometimes when I was really good or had done some small thing that Grandma thought was extra helpful, she would take me by the hand and we would visit her bedroom.

It was a small room, simply furnished with quaint redwood furniture. On top of her chest of drawers sat Grandmother's mysterious wooden wonder box. As a child, it looked so big to me with drawers cascading down the front. The best part of that box was when you opened the top, it stretched out like an awakening cat, and wonder of wonders—at least to my young and curious nature—it had a secret drawer.

With me in tow, Grandma would open the wonderful box, fumble with the little secret drawer, and hand me a dime. Then she would explain why I was getting that little gift and send me on my way.

In those days, a dime bought a lot. Baseball cards came two in a pack with a piece of gum for a couple of cents, and penny candy filled the grocery store's glass display cases. Saving a dime was a pretty good idea too. But it wasn't the money that was important. It was that Grandma, who had little, was giving something of value to tell me that I was important to her.

I don't know whatever happened to Grandma's box, but I think I have been searching for it most of my adult life. Maybe someday I will even find that very box or one like it. I'll look in the secret drawer and find a lone dime. In the meantime, each time I find a new addition to my collection, I imagine stories to go with it as I open it. I put little treasures inside of many of my boxes, hoping that when I die, my children or grandchildren will find each of them along with a little poem or picture that sends a heartfelt message to whomever hunts through my things.

In the long run, I think our lives are very similar to boxes. Each episode of our personal history as it flows along shows us something new or reinforces something He has been trying to teach us. When the lesson is partly or wholly learned, we often put it away in a memory container to ponder when needed and move on to our next lesson. Our stories, then, are metaphorically stored in different shaped or colored containers—colors of joy or sorrow, of laughter and tears. All of these life journeys fit like boxes into the compartments of our mind, a collection that sits there quietly waiting to be rediscovered. Our boxes of yesterday give us the reminiscences of tomorrow.

So I imagine I will always love boxes, and I guess I will always share boxes. I also believe that the wisdom I'm collecting in the boxes of my spirit are bringing me closer to the place where the Gift-Giver wants me to be. For I believe that the miracle of memory is more precious than gold.

> Let us not grow weary in well doing, for in due season we shall reap if we do not lose heart.
> (Galatians 6:9 RSV)

Prayer

Lord, what a journey life is. So many memories, so much stored in the computers of our brain. Sad events and happy ones, they are all there as You will, ready to surface when needed or desired. I find myself amazed that after many, many years, I can still see vividly a person who touched my life.

"How wonderful are your works," cries the psalmist in Psalm 139. Help us to live in wonder at the mystery of it all. Help us to gratefully lift our hearts in praise for the gift of memory. And in rejoicing over our gift, help us to remember to pray for those who have lost theirs. Amen.

Masterpiece

Wrinkle-faced woman
Petite, stoic icon of time well spent
Resting
on old wooden bench.
What stories live behind those kind eyes?
What thoughts travel in and out
As you sit there, gnarled hands folded in lap?
Quiet.
You—an artist's masterpiece,
Mysterious *madonna**
Posing
Amid flowers in the garden of life.
Picture-perfect
Etched
in the memory-box
Of some long-ago-child's mind.

*Meaning number two, obscure: an Italian lady (Webster's dictionary)

Note: Sometimes I feel it is important to see life from the eyes of a child. So I am adding this little story that, on the whole, explains a lot about how I am able to feel comfortable with our Heavenly Father. God blessed me with a dear dad. This story is a glimpse of that relationship.

My Father's Arms

> You are my hiding place; You will protect me from trouble and surround me with songs of deliverance. (Psalm 32:7 NIV)

One June day when I was very young, I ran out the door in my green and red plaid dress to explore the sights and sounds of early summer. Brown braids beat against my back as I scooted down the stone steps to the backyard. Bees buzzed around the tops of our flowers, and the grass glistened as green as emeralds with the last drops of dew. I wandered about the yard looking for my father, who, I supposed, had gone out to the garden after his chores and breakfast. Where had he gone?

Listening quietly, I heard the faint rumble of Dad's voice. It appeared to be coming from the home of our dear neighbor, Mr. Gilbert. Curiosity filled my mind, and I decided to follow the sound of his voice and see what was going on. I exited the backyard and bounded up to the garage. Pulling open the heavy door with all the strength a young child could muster, I grabbed my tall maroon tricycle.

In the 1940s, before smaller bicycles with training wheels became popular, many children graduated to a larger tricycle until they were ready to tackle a regular-size bike. I had inherited my big sister's. The front and back wheels were quite a bit larger than the common small tricycle of today, and the little vehicle actually moved right along. Thinking I could get to my father faster if I rode to our neighbor's, I climbed on the seat and barreled out of our driveway and off along the street in front of my house.

Coming to Mr. Gilbert's driveway, I made a right turn. It was downhill all the way to his garage. At the time, it seemed like a long and wonderful ride, with smooth bumps where the seams were set in the cement pavement. It was such a thrill to swoop down that drive. Coming toward the end, I quickly turned and drove to my neighbor's yellow porch steps. Alas, at this point, I made a choice that would change the course of the next few weeks.

Next to Mr. Gilbert's house, there was a huge yard and a giant garden. At my young age, it seemed to stretch on forever. The garden boasted an orchard of peaches and plums, as well as glorious, well-kept flower beds with beautiful, sweet-smelling roses. It was a dream to my big, little girl eyes. The garden was divided into sections, and between each section were double foot-wide boards so people could walk along and enjoy each of his masterpieces. The garden began at the end of a long downhill ramp. Right there stood my father and Mr. Gilbert in a deep discussion.

My fanciful imagination assumed they were talking about their mutual love of gardening.

Seeing my dad standing there amid the rose gardens, I happily decided to surprise him. I started pedaling down that boardwalk, which was certainly not designed for little girls on tricycles. Before I could grasp the situation, I had careened down the first narrow board at full speed, my feet no longer able to keep up with the pedals. Mr. Gilbert and my dad heard my surprised cry just in time as I sped down the little hill out of control. In shock, they jumped out of the way as an impetuous, pig-tailed little lady flew right past them. Suddenly, the tricycle caught on the edge of a board. I flew through the air and dropped while the wheeled villain crashed on top of me. There was a sudden burst of pain in my knee. That old tricycle was not much of a friend that day.

Tears of fear and anxiety streamed down my face. My knee felt like a gun had blasted it apart. I remember my father lovingly picking me up as I buried my head in his shoulder and wailed. The mixed smell of sweat and animals from his finished farm work was comforting. The feel of his gentle embrace is still etched in my memory. He took me home, and within a few hours, my knee had grown to a gigantic size. The doctor—they came to your house in those days—diagnosed "water on the knee," and I was relegated to leg rest and soaking my knee in Epsom salts for several days. I was told not to walk until I was sufficiently healed. Thus, I had to be carried from room to room. Guess who took the job—my gentle, comforting dad.

Nowadays my knee, still weak, reminds me of this time.

The older I get, the more accurate it becomes as a weather forecaster. More than that, however, this old injury has taught me much about life. My father's love taught me to easily trust in the love of my Heavenly Father. I learned that in the crises of my life, someone will always be there, someone who will hold me up and carry me through. I learned that although we may wear the scars of our foolish choices, what we learn from them is the clay that forms our lives into God's perfect shape for us. In the summers as I tend my beautiful rose gardens, I see this memory as one of the molds for shaping the person I turned out to be.

When I think of heaven, I most often picture the Lord in a garden. The old hymn "In the Garden" is one of my favorites. Just as I remember the love of my earthly father among the flowers next door, I anticipate meeting our Heavenly Father in His garden. After the cares of life are done, I imagine myself, bruised and broken and still impulsive, ready to rest in His arms.

> He will cover you with His pinions and under
> His wings you will find refuge; His faithfulness
> is a shield and a buckler. (Psalm 91:4 RSV)

Prayer

Well, Lord, here I am. Still a child at heart, always seeing the beauty around me with eyes of wonder. Still a child in the process of growing, wondering how long it will take me to learn all You want to teach me. Still a child struggling with those same old faults that resurface again and again to my chagrin. But oh how far I have come in these many years of laughter and tears.

Just know, Lord, that I am Yours to do with as You please and, Lord, thank You for the gift of sharing in story little glimpses of Your presence in my life with others. Amen.

Simple Games

Merriment, merriment flows all around
As laughter of children's play makes its sweet sound.
The running of races, the bouncing of balls,
The "Safe!" cry of baseball, the sobbing from falls.
The clicking and clacking of roller skate wheels,
And someone's pet puppy that nips at your heels.
There's hopscotch and jump rope and yo-yos to boot
And sweet little boys bearing snakes or a newt.
The catching of minnows in unsafe tin cans
Or finding that fossil for dinosaur fans.
The play of an era when simple was fun
In woods or in creeks, under shade or in sun.

Questions to Contemplate or Discuss:

1. Grandmothers and grandfathers are of primary importance in most of our lives. Share your memories and stories in your journal or in your study group.
2. How was your relationship with God influenced by something that happened in your life? Was it a positive event that took you toward the Lord or one that pushed you away? How are you dealing with this incident now?
3. Have the stories in this book made you remember the stories in your own life? Consider journaling some of your own stories, asking God whom you might share them with.
4. In your group or with a friend, remember the games you played as a child. Jot them down and compare notes. See if you share any of the same ones. Tell stories.

Scripture Readings and Reflections:

1Peter 5:1–5
Isaiah12
1John 2:1–14

Activities:

1. Work on a heritage album, using old pictures and other treasures that tell the history of your family. Be sure to write names and places so the next generation will continue your family story.
2. Make a box for each of your children or grandchildren that contains samples of what you treasure—for example, a copy of your favorite book or a piece of something you collect.

Personal Reflections:

Afterword

It has been a simple joy to put these ten stories together. While they are all different events with different people, they are the same in that they all urge the reader and me, the writer, to look at our storehouse of memories. They encourage us to stretch out of the tightness of our too stressful, too busy lives and look back to the many times God has touched us with a miracle, simple or profound.

In my first book, *Simpler Times: Reflections on Women's Friendship*, I hoped you would see in your relationships with friends how they molded you into God's special person, just as the women in my book did me. With this book, I wanted to take you a step further, leading you to think about your own stories and how God has tried to reach you through them. Perhaps you will desire to share with your family, a group, or a friend different memories that came to your mind as I have shared mine.

Life is an amazing adventure. We are unique in that each of us could be involved in the same incident and have a completely different perspective when we look back at it. You may read each of my stories and form an entirely different understanding that may have never entered my mind. That is the gift, the gift of our little piece of God's infinite tapestry. We are made in His image and His image is so vast that no two of us will ever be or think exactly alike. So go ahead, share!

-0-

About the Author

Kathleen (Kathy) McDonald started writing almost as soon as she learned to use a pencil. A graduate with bachelor's and master's degrees from the State University of New York at Cortland, she has taught for many years in public and private schools. While raising her children, she continued to write, keeping journals, as well as notebooks full of poetry. She has had several articles and poems published. In 2015, her first book, *Simpler Times: Reflections on Women's Friendship*, was published.

With her second book, *Simple Joys: Reflections of Life's Little Miracles*, Kathy hopes to satisfy her readers who asked for more and challenge them to share their own stories. Meanwhile she is working on several other manuscripts, including a poetry anthology and children's literature.

Kathy, a mother and grandmother, lives with her husband in Bath, New York. She is involved in her church and her Bible study group. She also paints and makes cards with a group called the Dippy Dabblers and delights in her many grandchildren. Books, music, film, scrapbooking, card making, and all things creative intrigue her as does gardening and travel.

Printed in the United States
By Bookmasters